52

Fun Family

Prayer

Adventures

52 Fun Family Prayer Adventures:

Creative Ways to Pray Together

Mike & Amy Nappa

Augsburg

MINNEAPOLIS

To our dear friends
Rick and Ellen Frandsen,
with whom we've shared many prayers
and many adventures!

52 FUN FAMILY PRAYER ADVENTURES
Creative Ways to Pray Together

Cover design by Marti Naughton
Interior design by David Meyer
Cover and interior illustrations by Stéphanie Roth

Library of Congress Cataloging-in-Publication Data

Nappa, Mike, 1963-
52 fun family prayer adventures : creative ways to pray together /
Mike & Amy Nappa
    p. cm.
  Includes bibliographical references and index.
  ISBN 0-8066-2841-3 (alk. paper)
  1. Family—Prayer-books and devotions—English. 2. Devotional calendars.
3. Spiritual life—Christianity. I. Nappa, Amy, 1963-. II. Title.
BV255.N38 1996
249—dc20
                   95-49167
                   CIP

Manufactured in the U.S.A.

AF 9-2841

00 99 98   2 3 4 5 6 7 8 9 10

Contents

Introduction 11

1. Breaking Through 14
   Obstacles to prayer

2. "ABC"'s of Adoration 15
   Adoration of God

3. Thanks for the Memories 16
   Thanking God for responding to prayers

4. Coins in a Fountain 18
   Forgiveness

5. God's Instructions 19
   Praying as the Bible directs

6. Prayers with Candy 21
   Praying for others

7. Playground Prayers 23
   Praying for children

8. Word of the Day 24
   Thanking God each day

9. Sunrise Watch 25
   A quiet time of thanks

10. Scripture Prayers 26
    Prayers from the Bible

11. Reflections of God in a Gallery of Praise 30
    God's creation

12. It's on the Map 32
    Praying for people we don't know

13. Friend of the Day 34
    Friends

14. Prayer Toss 36
    Prayer for family members

15. Penny Prayers 38
    The small miracles of life

16. Pantomime Prayers 40
    Communicating through actions

17. Seed Spittin' Prayer. 42
    Outdoor prayer time
18. Real Estate Prayer. 44
    Prayer for our home
19. Sponsored in Prayer. 45
    Caring for a child through prayer
20. I Remember. 46
    People and memories from the past
21. Puzzling Prayers 48
    Recognizing answered prayers
22. Wet-Head Prayers 50
    Praying for family members
23. Pray for Me When This You See 52
    Remembering needs of family members
24. Anywhere Prayer 53
    God hears us everywhere
25. Prayer Calendar 54
    A month of guided prayer
26. Bouquet of Blessings 56
    Flowers as symbols of prayer
27. In Motion. 58
    The Lord's Prayer
28. Porch Listen 59
    Praying for the world around us
29. Prayer Notebook 60
    Long-term prayer needs
30. Songs of Prayer 61
    Communicating through music
31. Fishing for Compliments 62
    Praising God
32. Make a Joyful Noise 64
    Laughter
33. Birds of Pray 65
    We are important to God
34. Book of Answered Prayers 66
    Recording prayers and praises
35. Lucky Number Seven. 68
    Enemies

36. Heavenly Hallelujahs. 70
    "The Hallelujah Chorus"

37. Little Reminders. 72
    Reminders to pray for each other

38. Sin Slam Dunk 75
    Forgiveness from each other and God

39. Musical Prayers 76
    Praying for each other

40. Prayers for Heroes 78
    People we admire

41. Gone with the Wind 80
    Saying you're sorry

42. Stations of Prayer. 82
    Different kinds of prayer

43. Finger Prayer 84
    A child's prayer

44. Outside-In Prayer. 85
    Family

45. Instrument of Prayer. 86
    Peace

46. Far from Home 88
    Remembering others in prayer

Prayer Adventures for Special Occasions

47. Birthday Candle Prayers 92
    Birthdays

48. Letters to God. 94
    Advent or New Year's

49. Out of the Darkness 96
    Good Friday or Easter

50. Star-Spangled Prayer. 98
    Independence Day

51. Travel Time with God 100
    Summer Vacation

52. Christmas Card Prayer. 101
    Remembering friends after Christmas

Index of Scripture References 103

Dear God,

My dad thinks he is you. Please straighten him out.

Wayne (age 11)

SOURCE: Talking to Your Child about God, by David Heller, pg. 32, published in 1987 by Perigree.

Introduction

We hate to admit but it, but sometimes we get bored by prayer. Don't get us wrong, prayer is one of the most powerful forces God has granted us on this earth. And it's certainly not God's fault if our minds wander during prayer. There should be nothing more appealing than spending time in prayer. The problem is, we still are sometimes bored by prayer. And we'll bet that, on occasion, you and your family get bored, too.

It happens all too often, whether you're praying alone or with others. Your head is bowed and you're ready to pray. Perhaps someone else is even praying aloud. Then . . . .

You lose your train of thought. You think about work. You think about the last song you heard on the radio. You think about the dog barking in the back yard, whether or not the mail will come early or late, whether or not you returned your library book in time to avoid a fine, if you'll be able to get in a few good spikes during the next volleyball game, and on and on. You've forgotten God is listening as you make a mental list of things you must do in the next few hours, days, or weeks.

We know, because we've been there. We find ourselves saying, "Well, we have to go pray," instead of "Wow! We get to go pray!" And this attitude has carried over into our times of family prayer. We quickly ramble through our requests as if reading a shopping list. Our time of thanks before a meal is a race to see if the prayer can be finished before someone starts to eat anyway.

But, instead of assuming that boredom during prayer must be endured, we decided to do something about it. The results were this book.

So What's In This Book Anyway?

In *52 Fun Family Prayer Adventures: Creative Ways to Pray Together* you'll find a collection of innovative ideas to help you and your family focus your prayers and add meaning to the

11

words you say. These ideas aren't meant to replace what you already do in prayers; they're intended to bring a change of pace to your existing prayer lives in a hands-on way.

Since we can talk to God any time and any place, we've included a wide variety of prayer adventures in this book. There are activities to be shared at dinner, to experience just before bedtime, for a Saturday morning, and that involve an outing for your family. Some of these adventures can be done alone, while others include the whole gang. We've also included a section of prayer adventures that correspond to holidays or special days.

As you read through the ideas in this book, you'll find that some ideas involve daily participation, while others involve projects that last for a week, a month, or even a year. Remember, you don't have to use these ideas all at once! Perhaps your family will choose one on-going prayer adventure that lasts a month. During this time you might want to include one or two "one-time" prayer adventures. And if your family really enjoys a specific adventure, use it again. Pick and choose the ideas that will work best for your family, or modify others to your liking.

Sprinkled throughout this book you'll also find tidbits of information on prayer, quotes from famous prayers, Scriptures about praying, and stories of answered prayers. Use these to inspire you, to challenge your thinking, to read aloud to your family, or whatever.

We want prayer to be an exciting part of our everyday lives, and we're hoping this book will make prayer an exciting part of your family life as well. Ready? Then turn the page for your first prayer adventure.

"Praise God from whom all blessings flow.
Praise him all creatures here below.
Praise him above ye heavenly host.
Praise Father, Son, and Holy Ghost."

SOURCE: Hymn—"Doxology"

Breaking Through

1.

Focus: Obstacles to prayer

For this adventure you'll need a large sheet of paper that will cover a doorway in your home. (You might use the blank side of gift wrap if necessary.) You'll also need a marker and tape.

Gather your family for a time of prayer. Read James 5:13-16 together and discuss why God wants us to talk to him.

Then ask, "What things keep you from praying?" As family members share their answers, write these on the large sheet of paper. Share your own reasons as well. Also ask family members what obstacles there are to your family taking time to pray together and write these on the paper.

When everyone has shared and all answers are written, tape the sheet of paper over an open doorway. Then ask your family members to join with you in breaking through these barriers to prayer. (Let younger children break through the paper first.) When everyone has gone through the doorway, gather together on the other side for a time of prayer. Pray that God will help your family overcome the obstacles they shared so that individually and together you can grow closer to God by communicating with him.

You may also want to take this time to plan a regular time to meet together for prayer. Many families pray together at meals, or before school, or before bedtime. If your family already prays at times like these, we encourage you to continue. But you may also want to set aside a short period of time one day a week, such as fifteen minutes every Sunday night, or the ten minutes following dinner on Mondays, where everyone can come together to share and pray. You'll find that many of the adventures in this book can be used during times such as these.

14

2

"ABC"s of Adoration

Focus: Adoration of God

Gather twenty-six sheets of paper, and label each page with one letter of the alphabet. Starting with the page labeled "A," have your family work together to list all of the things they admire about God that begin with the letter on that page.

For example, on the "A" page, family members might list things like:

- awesome power,
- affectionate love, and
- activity in my life.

The "B" page, might include:

- beautiful creation,
- blessings I've received, and
- the Bible that tells me about God.

Once your family has thought of at least one thing to write on each page, bind the twenty-six pages together for future use. You could put the pages in a notebook, or simply staple them together. Then use this book as a guide for family prayers. Open to one of the alphabet pages and begin your family's prayer by saying, "Lord, You are worthy to be adored. We know because of these things . . . " and read to God the list for that letter. Let family members take turns choosing a page from the book to pray through. As you and your family pray, explain why the items you listed are things you admire about God.

Keep this book in a convenient place. Encourage everyone to add new things they think of that they'd like to give God praise for, and include them in your prayers as well.

3.

Thanks for the Memories

Focus: Thanking God for responding to prayers

Start a box of memories in which you will collect mementos to remind you and your family of God's active presence in your lives.

Begin by taking a shoe box or other similar container and having family members decorate the outside of the box. (You can use items such as wrapping paper, construction paper, stickers, and markers.)

Then tell your family, "Each time we notice God working in response to one of our prayers, we'll find something that will remind us of what God has done and put it in this box." Give your family examples of what you mean, such as these:

• If a friend recovers from an illness, you might put a get-well card in the box.

• If God provides for you financially, you could drop a check stub in the box.

• If you pray for guidance and God leads you in a certain direction, you may want to add a compass or road map to the box.

• If you pray for help on a test and do well, you might want to put a page of your class notes into the box after the test!

After a week of collecting items in your memories box, gather together to look through the box. Use it to remind everyone of reasons for thanking God. Include in your prayer a time of thanksgiving when you open the box and take out the mementos one by one. As you examine each thing, have the family member who chose the item thank God for what it represents and for the way God has worked in his or her life in the past week.

At this point the box can be emptied and your family can start over, or you may wish to leave these mementos in the box to serve as long-term reminders of God's work. Continue to add to the box as often as you like, using it whenever you all need a reminder of how God has answered the prayers of your family.

4.

Coins in a Fountain

Focus: Forgiveness

Collect a handful of coins (pennies, nickels, dimes, or quarters will do) and place them in a small cup or other container. Take this cup and go with your family to a fountain for a time of prayer. (Check a local mall, library, or city building to find a fountain.)

As you stand or sit together in front of the fountain, pass the container of coins and have each person select one. Say, "This is a time for each of us to tell God we're sorry for things we've done wrong."

Then begin by praying, "Lord, in this past week I know I've disappointed you in this way . . ." and finish by confessing to God one way you've fallen short in your spiritual life. Then toss your coin into the water of the fountain. Encourage each family member to pray in the same manner, ending the prayer by tossing his or her coin into the fountain. If anyone is too embarrassed to share a confession aloud, allow him or her to pray silently before tossing a coin.

Repeat this confessing and coin-tossing process as many times as you like. When everyone is done, ask family members to dip their hands in the fountain's water for a quick washing.

Then close your family prayer by saying, "Thank you, God, for the promise of your forgiveness that buries our sins as this fountain has "buried" our coins, and that washes our hearts as this water has washed our hands. In Jesus' name. Amen."

God's Instructions

Focus: Praying as the Bible directs

This prayer adventure is great for families with kids in junior or senior high. During the next week, read a different passage from the following list each day. Discuss the questions together, then pray as you are directed in the Bible.

Day One: Psalm 122—The peace of Jerusalem

• What is the significance of Jerusalem in this passage?
• Why does the psalmist command the reader to "Pray for the peace of Jerusalem"?
• What meaning does this command have for us today?
• Pray according to what you have learned.

Day Two: Matthew 5:43-48 and Luke 6:27-36—Persecutors

• What prayer is commanded in these passages?
• Why is it important to pray for our enemies?
• Discuss and answer the questions raised in both passages.
• How can you bless an enemy?
• Pray as you are instructed.

Day Three: Mark 13:32-37—Watch and pray

• What is this passage discussing?
• Why is it necessary to be alert while praying?
• According to this passage, how should you be acting and praying?
• Let your prayers be guided by what you have discovered today.

Day Four: 2 Thessalonians 3:1-2 and Hebrews 13:18—Prayer for missionaries

- Who is requesting prayer in these passages and why?
- Who do you know in similar situations as the writers of these passages?
- How can your prayers help these people?
- Pray for these people as directed here.

Day Five: Matthew 9:35-38—Harvest

- What kind of harvest is Jesus referring to?
- Who are the workers that Jesus wants us to pray God will send?
- Are you a worker?
- Use this passage as a guide to prayer.

Day Six: Matthew 6:5-8—Pray in secret

- What different kinds of people are described here?
- Which are you most like and why?
- Today, pray individually, as this verse instructs.

Day Seven: Luke 18:1-8—Persistence in prayer

- What is the main point of this story?
- Why did Jesus tell it?
- In what areas do you need to be more persistent in prayer?
- Determine how to be consistent and persistent in your prayers, beginning today.

After the week of studying and obeying the Bible's instructions on prayer, what have you learned? If you like, continue this project by having family members find other references to prayer. (You may want to use a concordance or other reference books.) As you learn more about God's instructions for prayer, you may find your understanding of prayer and your actual prayers changing!

Prayers with Candy

Focus: Praying for others

Use M & M's ® candy to help focus your family's prayers of intercession for others.

Pass around a bag or bowl of M & M's the next time your family is gathered for prayer. Let each person take a handful, but don't let anyone eat the candies yet. Explain that the color of the candies will indicate the direction of the families' prayers. Lead your family in prayer using this guide and stopping for prayer after explaining each color. Say:

- "For every green M & M you chose, pray for your spouse (present or future) or some other significant person in your life." This is a great way to get kids thinking about what qualities they want to find in a future mate. Encourage them to pray for this person's safety, spiritual and physical growth, and so on.

- "For every red M & M you chose, pray for a member of our family by name (a parent, son, daughter, brother, sister, grandchild, niece, nephew, cousin, aunt, uncle, and so on)."

- "For every orange M & M you chose, pray for a teacher in your life (a supervisor, a professor, a pastor, a Bible study leader, a child's schoolteacher, a mentor, or another type of teacher)."

- "For every yellow M & M you chose, pray for one of your neighbors (a neighbor near your home, a co-worker, someone whose desk is near yours at school, or a neighbor close to your church)."

- "For every dark brown M & M you chose, pray for a leader in your life (a politician, a local businessperson, a celebrity, a member of your church's staff, the President, or another leader)."

- "For every light brown M & M you chose, pray for Christians in other countries."

This might be best used as an after dinner prayer time. Repeat this process as often as your family's calorie intake allows!

"Make my life a prayer to you.
I want to do what you want me to,
No empty words and no white lies,
No token prayers, no compromise."

—Keith Green

SOURCE: Song— "Make My Life a Prayer to You," by Keith Green, from *Keith Green: The Ministry Years*, vol. 1, disk 2.

Playground Prayers

Focus: Praying for children

Visit a nearby playground or park where children gather to play. If your children want, allow them to join in the activities of the playground. Then sit in an inconspicuous spot and simply watch the kids for awhile as they run and tumble and laugh and cry.

When you're ready, begin praying for a specific child on the playground. Use what you see in that child as a tool to focus your prayer.

For example, if you notice a child is particularly adventurous and prone to take risks, pray that God would channel that adventuresome spirit into ways that would lead to the child discovering more about God. (You might also pray for that child's safety and protection!)

Or, if you notice a child who often plays alone and seems disconnected from the other kids, you might pray that God would surround that child with people who can become deep, meaningful friends.

If you spot a child who is unkind, you could pray that God will change the heart of that person to become one that seeks God and takes an interest in others.

If your children are playing as well, pray specifically for each one. If your children are sitting with you, have them join you in praying for those playing nearby, being sure they have a chance to talk to God about the children they see.

As you pray, ask God to direct your prayers for each child. Finish your time with a prayer for all the children you see to experience God's love in a tangible way throughout the rest of their lives. Pray for as many children as time allows.

8.

Word of the Day

Focus: Thanking God each day

Begin this prayer adventure on the last day of a month. Before you begin, gather a jar, a pen, and twenty-eight to thirty-one slips of paper.

Tell your family, "Let's brainstorm one thing we can thank God for each day of this next month." For example, if the upcoming has thirty days, you'll want to come up with thirty things to thank God for over the next month.

Work together to brainstorm one thing to write on each slip of paper. Also, be sure to include the names of each family member among the slips of paper.

When you have the desired number, fold the paper slips and place them in the jar. On the following morning, ask one family member to reach into the jar and select a slip of paper. Read the word aloud to everyone, then tape the paper in a place where everyone will see it (such as on the refrigerator door or the bathroom mirror). For this entire day let your thoughts of thanks to God include what is written on the slip of paper.

The next morning, take down the previous day's item of thanks and have another family member select a new slip of paper. Repeat this each day of the month until all the slips of paper have been used and God has been thanked repeatedly for each one!

24

Sunrise Watch

Focus: A quiet time of thanks

This prayer adventure may be the most difficult one in this entire book—it requires getting up before the sun! If you can entice your whole family out of bed before the crack of dawn (do we smell bacon sizzling?), include everyone in this time of prayer. Or you may want to use it on a special occasion when two family members are up early for a fishing expedition or when a parent is still up after soothing a sick child through the night.

If all else fails, you could use this idea during a sunset instead.

Here's what to do: Find a place where you can see the sunrise clearly. If the view from your windows isn't good, try a park, a scenic overlook, or even your roof (if you're careful). Then settle down to watch the first rays of dawn peak through the dark.

Each time you see a new color in the sky, thank God for something beautiful. For example, as pink glows in the sky, thank God for the smile of a friend. As the sky turns orange, thank God for the sweet friendship of family members. As yellow shines through, thank God for the beauty of a favorite flower. Continue in your time of thanks until the sun is shining brightly.

Then head to breakfast with a smile of thanksgiving on your face!

Note: Because looking directly into the sun can damage vision, be sure to caution children to look at the sky around the sun—not directly at the sun itself.

10.

Scripture Prayers

Focus: Prayers from the Bible

Copy each of the following scripture passages onto a 3 x 5 card and place them in a stack on your dining room table.

• Psalm 9:1-2

"I will praise you, O LORD, with all my heart; I will tell of all your wonders. I will be glad and rejoice in you; I will sing praise to your name, O Most High."

• Psalm 25:1-5

"To you, O LORD, I lift up my soul; in you I trust, O my God. Do not let me be put to shame, nor let my enemies triumph over me. No one whose hope is in you will ever be put to shame, but they will be put to shame who are treacherous without excuse. Show me your ways, O LORD, teach me your paths; guide me in your truth and teach me, for you are God my Savior, and my hope is in you all day long."

• Matthew 6:9b-13

"Our Father in heaven,
hallowed be your name,
your kingdom come, your will be done
on earth as it is in heaven.
Give us today our daily bread.
Forgive us our debts,
as we also have forgiven our debtors.
And lead us not into temptation,
but deliver us from the evil one."

• Ephesians 3:14-17a

"For this reason I kneel before the Father, from whom his whole family in heaven and on earth derives its name. I pray that out of his glorious riches he may strengthen you with power through his Spirit in your inner being, so that Christ may dwell in your hearts through faith."

• Ephesians 3:17b-19

"And I pray that you, being rooted and established in love, may have power, together with all the saints, to grasp how wide and long and high and deep is the love of Christ, and to know this love that surpasses knowledge—that you may be filled to the measure of all the fullness of God."

• 1 Samuel 2:2

"There is no one holy like the LORD; there is no one besides you; there is no Rock like our God."

• 2 Samuel 7:22

"How great you are, O Sovereign LORD! There is no one like you, and there is no God but you, as we have heard with our own ears."

• Habakkuk 3:2

"LORD, I have heard of your fame; I stand in awe of your deeds, O LORD. Renew them in our day, in our time make them known."

• Psalm 42:1-2a

"As the deer pants for streams of water, so my soul pants for you, O God. My soul thirsts for God, for the living God."

• Amos 5:24

"But let justice roll on like a river, righteousness like a never-failing stream!"

- **Psalm 51:10,12**

"Create in me a pure heart, O God, and renew a steadfast spirit within me. . . . Restore to me the joy of your salvation and grant me a willing spirit, to sustain me."

- **Psalm 61:1-3**

"Hear my cry, O God; listen to my prayer. From the ends of the earth I call to you, I call as my heart grows faint; lead me to the rock that is higher than I. For you have been my refuge, a strong tower against the foe."

- **Psalm 86:11**

"Teach me your way, O LORD, and I will walk in your truth; give me an undivided heart, that I may fear your name."

- **Psalm 145:1-2**

"I will exalt you, my God the King; I will praise your name for ever and ever. Every day I will praise you and extol your name for ever and ever."

Before your evening meal, have each family member who knows how to read take a card from the top of the stack. Then take turns reading these prayers from the Bible aloud. If the words or phrases are too difficult for younger children in your family to understand, talk together about what the verse means. Let these words from God's word be your mealtime prayer. If you like, spend time during your meal discussing the prayers from the Bible and how they express your own thoughts today.

When your prayer is over, return the cards to the stack to be used with another meal. As you and other family members discover other prayers in the Bible that are meaningful to your lives, add them to the stack of cards. The book of Psalms is full of prayers with a wide variety of meanings (praising God, thanking God, asking for help, and so on). It's a great place to have family members look for more verses if you'd like to add to your stack!

"God shapes the world by prayer.
The more praying there is in the world,
the better the world will be."

—E. M. Bounds

SOURCE: *Purpose in Prayer*, by E. M. Bounds, pg. 7, published by Moody Press.

11.

Reflections of God in a Gallery of Praise

Focus: God's creation

The Apostle Paul declared in Romans 1:20, "For since the creation of the world God's invisible qualities—his eternal power and divine nature—have been clearly seen, being understood from what has been made."

Every created thing reflects God's glory and power—so why not use God's creation to inspire your family's praise of God? Set up an area in your home (such as a bookshelf or the fireplace mantel) to place things that somehow reflect God's glory to you and your family. Then encourage family members to fill this area with things they find that inspire them to praise God.

For example, your family might fill your chosen spot with things like these:

- dried flower petals
- pictures of your family
- a bird's nest
- a puppy's collar
- a card with a favorite scripture verse written on it
- a small musical instrument
- a postcard from the Grand Canyon
- a valentine
- a child's drawing
- a pinecone
- a letter from a friend

Work together as a family to arrange the chosen items into a miniature "art gallery of God's praise," creating small "exhibits" for each one.

When your gallery of praise is ready, gather around and look through it while you pray together. Include in your prayers moments when family members tell God, "Lord, I see your glory in the things you've created. In this (name something from your gallery), I see your (name a character quality of God, such as love, patience, grace, beauty, and so on)."

You may also want to ask God to help your family members be good stewards of the gifts God has given us in creation. We can express our thanks for what God has made by our actions of caring for the world around us.

Feel free to add to and remove items from your family's gallery. This will help everyone find fresh new reasons for praising God in their prayers.

12.

It's on the Map

Focus: Praying for people we don't know

Purchase a map of the world or the country in which you live, then attach this map to a bulletin board.

Next, give each family member a dart and then take turns throwing darts at the map. (Older family members may want to help younger children do this safely.) Have family members pray for people who live in the areas that have been "pinpointed" by the darts.

For example, if a dart hits Colorado on the map, everyone can pray for the people of this state. The more detailed your map is, the more specific you can be as to which areas you pray for. Be sure to explain a bit about the area you're praying for to younger family members who don't yet have much knowledge of geography.

If you like, have family members do a bit of research about the areas in which the darts stick. Make a trip together to the local library and use encyclopedias, newspapers, and magazines to learn more about the countries, states, or cities you've pinpointed. Perhaps there's been war or political unrest, or a natural disaster. Or you may find the area to be enjoying wonderful weather and a low crime rate! Use the information to pray and offer praises more specifically for the people living there.

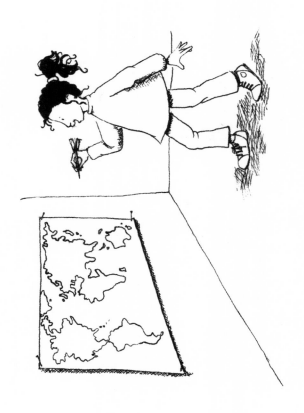

Variation: If you're uncomfortable using pointed darts with your children, you may want to try damp suction darts. Or young children may enjoy spinning a globe and letting their finger drag along the surface until the globe stops. Then they can pray for the people in the area where their finger is resting.

13.

Friend of the Day

Focus: Friends

Each night as you pray with your child before bed, include one of your child's friends in your prayers. Let your child choose which friend he or she would like to pray for. Some children will enjoy selecting friends randomly, while others may want to create a list or even cover a bulletin board with pictures of friends to use as a reference. Allow the decision of who to pray for to be your child's. If he or she chooses the same friend for several nights in a row, that's fine.

If your child would like, have him or her pray aloud for the chosen friend. Or take turns praying for the friend. Here are ideas of how to pray:

- Pray for the child's spiritual growth. In a child's words, "Help (friend) to know you love him. Thank you that he learns about you at church." Or, "Help me show (friend) that you love her. Even though her family doesn't know about you, I pray that she learns about you from me and other people who know you."

- Pray for the child's safety.

- Pray for specific needs of the child as you are aware of them. "Jesus, watch over (friend) as she takes a test tomorrow." Or, "Help Kyle to get over his cold."

- Pray for the relationship between this child and your child. Thank God for giving your child friends. Ask God to help your child be an example of God's love to his or her friend.

- You may occasionally ask your child to pray for another child he or she doesn't consider a friend. This could be a school bully or another person the child doesn't care for. Pray that God will show his love to this child as well. You may also pray for an improved relationship between your child and this one.

"What a friend we have in Jesus,
  all our sins and grief's to bear!
  What a privilege to carry
  everything to God in prayer!"

—Joseph Scriven

SOURCE: Hymn—"What a Friend We Have in Jesus,"
  by Joseph Scriven and Charles C. Converse.

14.

Prayer Toss

Focus: Prayer for family members

Use this idea when your family is gathered for a time of prayer together. You'll need a sheet of paper and pencil for each person. Have each family member write his or her name and a request for prayer on his or her paper. (Ask older children to help younger ones who are non-readers.) The prayer requests can be for anything this family member feels is important. When everyone is ready, stand in a circle and say, "Crumple your paper and toss it up in the air so it falls into the center of the circle."

Wait to see where each paper wad lands. Then have family members pick up the paper nearest to where they are standing. Say, "Pray for the person whose paper you picked up."

If you like, spend time with each person silently praying over the request they have read, then re-crumple the papers and repeat the activity and time of prayer. Let everyone know it's okay to pray for the same person twice, or even to pray for your own request.

After doing this several times, have each person save the paper they picked up on the last toss and use it as a reminder to pray for the appropriate family member over the next week.

"The prayer of a righteous man is powerful and effective. Elijah was a man just like us. He prayed earnestly that it would not rain, and it did not rain on the land for three and a half years. Again he prayed, and the heavens gave rain, and the earth produced its crops."

—**The apostle James** (as quoted in James 5:16b-18)

15.

Penny Prayers

Focus: The small miracles of life

Many times we fail to notice what God is doing around us. We might forget to thank God for an answered prayer, or may simply not pay attention to the small miracles of safety, life, and beauty around us. This prayer adventure serves as a way to be sure God gets all the "credit."

Place an empty jar where it can be easily seen in your home. Then gather your family and say, "Each time you see God's hand at work in answer to a prayer, put a penny in this jar." (You may want to supply each person with a handful of pennies.) Explain that a penny could be placed in the jar when:

- A prayer is answered.

- You see a change in a person or situation and know God is working to make that change.

- You are kept safe in a dangerous situation.

- Your attitude is one of joy even in a difficult time or situation.

Have family members think of other examples of God being at work when a penny might be put into the jar. Then briefly pray, asking God to help family members be aware of God's hand throughout the week.

After a week, gather again to see how many pennies have been placed in the jar. Count the pennies, then have each person tell about one or two times he or she put a coin into the jar. Spend a few minutes thanking God for the riches of answered prayer and for reminding your family that God is always at work!

Return the jar to its spot for the upcoming week. After the jar has a good amount of pennies in it, allow your children to choose a way to use the coins to purchase a gift for someone. For example, kids might want to buy one or two flowers for a neighbor, or a can of food for a local soup kitchen.

A prayer of **King David** (as recorded in Psalm 5:1-2) . . . .

"Give ear to my words, O LORD,
consider my sighing.
Listen to my cry for help, my King and my God,
for to you I pray."

16.

Pantomime Prayers

Focus: Communicating through actions

When your family gathers to pray, have each person think of one prayer or praise they would like to express to God. Then say, "Think of a way to pantomime, or act out without using words, your thoughts to God. For example, if you want to apologize to God for doing the wrong thing, you might kneel and cover your face with your hands. If you want to thank God for being at work in your life, you might stand and applaud."

Give everyone a moment of "think time." Then your family can proceed in its prayer time in one of these ways:

1. Everyone can pantomime their thoughts to God at the same time. In this way, each person is concerned only with his or her own prayer.

2. One family member can begin by sharing his or her prayer and how it can be expressed. Then the entire family can pantomime the prayer of this person, corporately praying without words. Next, another family member can share and again pantomime your prayers as directed by this person.

When this time of prayer is over, discuss with your family another way to express thanks to God in pantomime. Close your time of prayer by offering thanks together using this physical expression.

Seed Spittin' Prayer

Focus: Outdoor prayer time

Use this prayer adventure during the hot summer months when everyone wants to be outdoors. You'll need a watermelon, a knife, and sidewalk chalk.

Draw a large "tic-tac-toe" board on your driveway or other cement surface. In four of the nine squares write the following words:

- Thanks
- Praise
- Forgive
- Help

Explain to your family members the meaning of each word:

"Thanks" is simply thanking God for something he has done.

"Praise" is telling God something good about himself, such as "God, you are powerful!"

"Forgive" means to ask God to forgive you for something you've done wrong.

"Help" is to ask God for help in some area of your life.

Then have your family members choose other words to fill in the remaining five squares. You may want to write the names of family members, friends, teachers, church staff members, and so on. Or you may choose other words, like *vacation, sunshine, the Bible,* and so on.

When each square has a word written in it, cut the water-melon and give each person a large slice. Have everyone stand or sit nearby the chalked tic-tac-toe board.

Say, "Spit your seeds onto this tic-tac-toe board. Wherever your seed lands, pray as the words direct. For example, if your seed lands on 'Praise,' tell God something great about himself. If it lands on a person's name, thank God for that person or pray for God to help that person."

Let this be a fun time of spitting seeds and praying one-sentence prayers aloud. Keep the prayers and seeds going as long as the watermelon lasts! Then get out the hose and wash the seeds and chalk away.

Real Estate Prayer

Focus: Prayer for our home

This prayer adventure will take your family on a walking tour of the place you live. As you gather for a time of prayer, explain that you'll be moving through each room of the house or apartment and praying for the people and activities represented by that room.

Begin in your living room. Pray for the time family members spend together in this room. Ask God to let those who visit in this room be aware of his love. Let any family member pray who wants to pray in this room. Then move on to the next room.

When you arrive at the bedrooms, pray for those who sleep there. Pray in specific ways for each person and for God's blessing upon those who come into this room each day. In the kitchen pray for family times together at meals. Ask that these be times of laughter and harmony. Thank God for the gift of food. Continue through your home, including areas such as the front entry, hallways, and so on. You might even want to include things such as your lawn, garage or parking stall, apartment swimming pool, and other areas as you like. Thank God for his provision of a home, and ask that this home would be a place where people experience God's love.

Close your time together by reading Joshua 24:15b, "As for me and my household, we will serve the Lord." Ask God to help everyone in your household serve him no matter what room they are in! If your family enjoys this prayer adventure, plan another time to travel to places where your family members spends time. Get into the car and drive to places like the baby-sitter's house, each child's school, workplaces of family members, and so on. At each place park the car for a couple of minutes and pray for the person who spends time there and for the activities that take place in that building.

19.

Sponsored in Prayer

Focus: Caring for a child through prayer

You've probably seen advertisements to sponsor a child financially through a relief organization. Perhaps your family even has "adopted" a child in another country through one of these charities. In this adventure, your family will sponsor a child through prayer for a year.

First, talk together and choose a child your family would like to support in prayer. If you do sponsor a child through a relief organization, perhaps you could choose that child. Or it could be a neighbor, a child you've read about in the newspaper, a child at school, a missing child, or any other child your family feels is in need of regular prayer.

If possible, obtain a picture of your chosen child and keep it on your refrigerator or another noticeable location. If a picture isn't available, select another object that will represent this person to your family. You might choose a small flag from the country where the child lives. Or if your chosen child is in need of medical attention, you might use a get-well card as your reminder.

Over the next year, pray regularly for this child. Make your prayers as specific as possible using any information you have access to. If it's appropriate, your family may also want to send cards or notes of encouragement or make other similar gestures to show your love and concern for this child.

After a year, thank God for any changes you've seen in this child. Then let your family decide if they'd like to continue praying for this child, or if they'd like to choose another child to pray for during the coming year.

20.

I Remember

Focus: People and memories from the past

Pull out the old photo albums and take a trip down memory lane! Gather everyone on the couch or a bed and reminisce about trips taken, past holidays, special events, and other occasions. Take your time looking through the pages and allow different family members to tell their memories of when each picture was taken.

Soon you'll be hearing things like, "That was the Christmas Mom had the flu and we got to order pizza!" and "Remember when Mr. Cunningham lived next door and we used to eat the strawberries from his garden? Does anyone know what ever happened to him?"

As you think of events and friendships, stop occasionally to pray. When pictures remind you of a fun vacation or wild adventure, thank God for the time you were able to spend together and the memories that were shared during that time. If a snapshot brings back memories of a hard time financially, or the death of a loved one or other difficult times, thank God for bringing you through that time and for being there with you. Ask God to continue to heal old wounds. Thank God for the lives and memories you have of deceased loved ones.

When you come upon pictures of long-lost friends, pray that God will continue to show himself to these friends. You may even want to find a person you'd forgotten about to ask forgiveness for a past wrong or to share with this friend about God's love. Or if friends pictured are still an active part of your lives, ask God to build your friendships and thank him for putting these people in your lives.

You may find pictures of family members no longer living with you, such as a daughter gone away to college. For some, this

46

could be those who have left because of divorce or other family separation. Remember to thank God for these people and to bring their needs before him as well.

As you talk with each other and God, don't forget to thank God for each other and for the time that you have to spend together right now!

"Before our Father's throne we pour our ardent prayers;
our fears, our hopes, our aims are one,
our comforts and our cares."

—John Fawcett

SOURCE: Hymn—"Blest be the Tie that Binds," by John Fawcett and Johann G. Nageli.

Puzzling Prayers

Focus: Recognizing answered prayers

For this prayer adventure you'll need a jigsaw puzzle. Choose the size and difficulty of your puzzle according to the ages and abilities of your family members. If your children are preschool aged, a puzzle with 30 to 40 pieces will work best. For school-age children and older, choose a puzzle with 50 to 150 pieces. (You probably won't want a puzzle with more than 150 pieces.)

Place the puzzle pieces and a pen on a card table or other flat surface where the puzzle can be left for a period of time. Then explain to your family that this puzzle will be put together as prayers are answered in your home.

Here's how it works:

Every time a person in your family realizes that God has answered a prayer, this person should choose a puzzle piece. On the back of the puzzle piece, the person should write a word or two (depending on the size of the piece) as a reminder of what the answer to prayer was.

For example, "A+" might be an answer to a prayer for help on a spelling test. "Sweet dreams" might mean a child's prayers not to have nightmares was answered. Or "$" could remind a college student (or the student's parents) that God provided money to make the tuition payment this month.

When two puzzle pieces have been written on, they can be attached together. Leave the puzzle pieces out until each piece has something written on the back and has been attached to the rest of the puzzle.

When the puzzle is complete, have your family admire the finished product. Then thank God for being involved in your family's prayers. Thank God for using your prayers to demonstrate the greater picture of his power.

If you like, leave the puzzle on display for a while as a reminder of all the prayers God has answered. Then take the puzzle apart and store it for later use. When you do pull it out see if family members can remember what the answers to prayer were by the notes written on each puzzle piece.

A prayer of **King David** (as recorded in Psalm 51:1-2, 10) . . .

"Have mercy on me, O God,
according to your unfailing love;
according to your great compassion
blot out my transgressions.
Wash away all my iniquity
and cleanse me from my sin. . . .
Create in me a pure heart, O God,
and renew a steadfast spirit within me."

Wet-Head Prayers

Focus: Praying for family members

Save this adventure for a hot summer day! Prepare by filling several small balloons with water. Place your supply of water balloons in a bucket or other container. Have your family meet outside in your yard or in a local park.

Ask your family to stand in a circle. (If only two people are participating, they should face each other.) Give each person a water balloon. Explain that on the count of three, everyone should throw his or her balloon into the air and try to catch a different balloon. Then count to three and let the balloon soar and the water splash! Continue tossing the balloons into the air until a balloon is broken.

As soon as a balloon breaks, stop the tossing and together determine who got the wettest. Then have another family member pray for this person. The prayer can be short, but it should focus on thanking God for this person and naming qualities others find special, or on specific requests this family member has shared.

Then "arm" everyone with balloons and begin tossing them again. Each time one or more balloons break, see who gets the wettest and pray for this person. It's okay to pray for the same person more than once. Also, encourage different family members to pray each time.

You may find it necessary to "bomb" a family member who continues to remain dry. Remember, everyone needs prayer!

When everyone is thoroughly soaked, pass out the towels and head inside. Then next time it's sunny, see if anyone wants to be refreshed again with a cooling prayer!

23.

Pray for Me When This You See

Focus: Remembering needs of family members

The next time your family is gathered together, ask each person to think of an item that could regularly be used to represent him or her. This should be an item that can be used again and again, and that other family members would associate with its owner. For example, a younger family member might have a special teddy bear or other stuffed animal that could be used as his or her representative item. A book lover might use a team hat or pennant. A sports fan might choose a favorite CD or cassette case.

When each person has chosen an item, have everyone show what their item is and, if necessary, explain why this item was chosen. Then determine together a spot that everyone sees daily. This could be a coffee table, mantle, kitchen counter, or other similar spot. Name this space the "Prayer Spot."

Then tell your family, "For the next month, whenever you feel like you need us to pray for you, put your item in the Prayer Spot to remind the rest of us that you need prayer." Thus, if Anthony is headed to the doctor for a shot, he might put his stuffed camel in the Prayer Spot. Or if Mom is making a special presentation at work, she might put her coffee mug in the Prayer Spot.

As the days of the month progress, be sure to pray for those who put their representative items in the Prayer Spot. If you like, leave a small note pad at the Prayer Spot so people can specify why they need prayer. Or ask family members to explain their need for prayer during a meal or other time you regularly gather. This will help others to pray more specifically.

On your own, or during times when the family is together, encourage family members to share how God has used the prayers of your family.

52

Anywhere Prayer

Focus: God hears us everywhere

This prayer adventure is fun for families with young children. With your children, read Psalm 139:1-4. Talk together about the meaning of this passage: God knows everything about us, including our thoughts. Then read verses 7-12. These verses say there is no place we can go where God is not there.

As you discuss this with your family, ask, "Can you think of any place we could go where God would not be and would not hear our prayers?"

Take your family into a closet or other cramped and dark space. Ask, "Do you think God can hear us here?" Assure them that the Bible says God will hear us anywhere, then pray right there, thanking God for hearing you.

Then ask your kids to think of another place to go. This might be the car, the basement, or in the backyard shed. Go to as many places as your children want, squish in together, and pray!

This adventure is especially reassuring to young children who are afraid of being alone or in the dark. God can always hear them, and they can talk to him wherever they are!

25.

Prayer Calendar

Focus: A month of guided prayer

This adventure will guide your family through a month of prayer. For each day of the following month, refer to the appropriate date given here, and pray as directed. If you like, copy the directions onto a large wall calendar and use this to help your family remember to pray each day.

Family members may wish to refer to the prayer calendar on their own, or you might share the topic of prayer at a specified time (such as at breakfast or dinner) and pray together each day for the month.

1. Thank God for each person living in your house.

2. Pray for your teacher, supervisor, or another person of authority.

3. Pray for an elderly person who lives alone.

4. Thank God for a special friend.

5. Ask God's forgiveness for things you have done wrong.

6. Sing a song (alone or as a family) that tells God how great he is.

7. Pray for the President of the country.

8. Thank God for an extended family member (like a grandparent or cousin).

9. Read Psalm 66:1-4 together, then shout to God, "How awesome are your deeds!"

10. Thank God for a person who makes your life difficult.

11. Pray for your neighbors.

12. Thank God for the comforts of your life such as food, a home, and clothing.

13. Ask God to show each person in your family his love in a special way today.

14. Tell God you're sorry for not always obeying him, and thank him for loving you still.

15. Pray for someone you've read about in the newspaper or heard about on the news.

16. Thank God for his creation and tell him one way you'll take care of it.

17. Pray for the leaders of your church such as Sunday school teachers, pastors, and youth leaders.

18. Tell God how much you appreciate his love.

19. Thank God for giving us the Bible.

20. Pray for the missionaries that you or your church supports. Also pray for the people they are reaching in their ministry.

21. Ask God to help you show love to each person you talk to today.

22. Pray for people who are living in an area torn by war. Ask God to restore peace to that land.

23. Pray for someone who is sick or sad.

24. Praise God for sending his Holy Spirit.

25. Pray for your co-workers, school-mates and/or others you come into contact with daily.

26. Thank God for your parents.

27. Ask God to help you grow closer to him.

28. Pray for the staff at your church, such as secretaries, custodians, and so on.

29. Tell God how much you appreciate his forgiveness.

30. Ask God to help you show kindness to others today.

31. Thank God for the wonderful gift of Jesus.

Bouquet of Blessings

Focus: Flowers as symbols of prayer

Traditionally, different flowers have symbolized a variety of emotions and messages. The following is a list of meanings that have been given in the past to these popular flowers:

- rose—*love*
- white chrysanthemum—*truth*
- white daisy—*innocence*
- gladiolus—*strength of character*
- iris—*message*
- ivy—*friendship*
- lily of the valley—*happiness*
- marigold—*grief*
- violet—*faithfulness*
- zinnia—*thoughts of absent friends*

Visit your local florist and collect a variety of these flowers. Then when you later gather with your family for a time of prayer, give each person one or more of the flowers. Share the meanings of the flowers, then ask each person to pray according to the meaning of their flower. For example,

- A person with a iris could thank God for the message of love he sent through Jesus, or God's message that we read in the Bible.

- If someone has a marigold, they could pray for others who are experiencing grief because of sickness, loss of a loved one, or other difficult times.

- The holder of a rose could thank God for his love, thank God for the love of family members, or ask God to help family members to show love to each other and those outside of the family.

Let family members think of different ways to use the symbolism of their flower to express thoughts of thanks, praise, and need to God. When your time of prayer is over, gather the flowers into a bouquet to be placed in your dining room or living room as a reminder of the prayers you have offered. Or give the bouquet as a gift to someone for whom you have prayed.

If your family enjoys this adventure, ask your florist or librarian for a book or two explaining the meaning of more plants. Use these as a guide to choosing bouquets of blessing!

27.

In Motion

Focus: The Lord's Prayer

Read Luke 11:1-4 with your family. Talk about what the words and phrases of this prayer mean. Then have your family members work together to create motions that express the meaning of the prayer.

For example, your family might express the word "hallowed" by making motions like the washing of hands, as this word means holy or pure. At "lead us not into temptation" you might hold your hands beside your eyes as if they were blinders. The younger your children are, the more concrete or realistic your actions will need to be. Older children may enjoy creating more abstract actions to express the words and phrases.

When you've created actions to express the entire prayer, say the prayer aloud together, making the appropriate motions. As you practice this prayer, you'll soon be able to use only the motions to express the thoughts in the prayer:

"Father,
hallowed be your name,
your kingdom come.
Give us each day our daily bread.
Forgive us our sins,
for we also forgive everyone who
sins against us.
And lead us not into temptation.'"

Porch Listen

Focus: Praying for the world around us

Take your family outside and sit together on your porch, patio, or backyard. If you don't have an area such as these, go to a local park, spread a blanket, and sit together.

Tell your family to listen quietly to the sounds around. After three to five minutes of quiet, say, "Now let's talk to God about the different sounds we hear."

Then begin with short, sentence prayers as you are guided by the sounds around you. For example,

- Pray for the neighbor children whose voices you hear.

- Thank God for all creation as you listen to crickets chirping.

- As you hear birds singing, thank God for music.

- If you hear the siren of a fire engine, pray for the safety of those who are waiting for help.

Finish by thanking God for each family member, as you've heard each other's voices.

Prayer Notebook

Focus: Long-term prayer needs

For this adventure you'll need a separate picture of each family member. Give each person his or her picture, along with a blank sheet of notebook paper and a pen or pencil. Have family members tape or glue their pictures to the top of the paper.

Ask family members to write two or three ongoing prayer requests that they have. These should be requests or goals that will need prayer for the next three to six months. For example:

• A parent may have an ongoing request for patience.

• A child may be in need of prayer in a continuously difficult school subject.

• Someone may be in need of healing of a long-term illness or condition.

Help younger family members write their requests. When the papers are completed, gather them together and place them in a notebook. Then place the notebook on a coffee table or other convenient location. Each day, turn the page to a different family member's page. You can pray together as a family for the pictured person, or leave the book out for those who pass by to see as a reminder to pray.

Update the pages every six months or so. If you like, tell extended family members (aunts, uncles, grandparents, cousins) what you're doing, and have them send pictures and request pages to be added to your book as well.

30.

Songs of Prayer

Focus: Communicating through music

Have each family member choose a hymn or praise song that expresses a theme about which they'd like to pray. For example, if someone is thankful that Jesus is his or her best friend, that person might choose "What a Friend We Have in Jesus." A person who is thankful for the love expressed through your own family or the church family could select "Blest Be the Tie That Binds." A family member wanting to praise God's glory might choose "Oh, for a Thousand Tongues to Sing." Even the youngest family members can participate with songs like "Jesus Loves Me," and "His Banner Over Me is Love."

It may be helpful to have a couple of hymnals or song books on hand for family members to use as reference. Or let younger kids look through their collection of cassette tapes or CDs to find a song that expresses their thoughts. Some family members might enjoy the challenge of writing an original song or writing new words to a familiar tune.

When everyone has chosen a song, start with the youngest person and take turns sharing what your song is and why you've selected it. Tell how this song expresses your thoughts, thanks, or praises to or about God.

Then sing each song as a prayer to God! If any family members play musical instruments, have them accompany you. Or sing along with a tape or CD. You could also sing your prayers a cappella.

Fishing for Compliments

Focus: Praising God

For this adventure you'll need to make a fishing pole. Tie about two or three feet of string to a stick such as a tree branch or a yardstick. At the end of the string tie a hook made from a paper clip.

Then take the cardboard roll from an empty roll of toilet paper or paper towels. Cut this into five to ten circles. (It's okay if they get a little bent in the cutting process.)

Gather your family together and ask everyone to think of things they'd like to compliment God on. These might be the great job he did making flowers, the gift of his love, his incredible power, and so on. As family members think of compliments for God, write each compliment on the outside of a different cardboard circle. When you've used all the circles, place them in a pile on the floor. Pass the fishing pole around and let each person "fish" for a cardboard circle. (For younger children, be sure the rolls are standing on their sides for easier hooking. Also, shorten the string by rolling it around the stick a few times.)

When each person has fished for and caught a compliment, take turns telling God how wonderful he is. Then continue fishing and complimenting until all the cardboard rolls are gone.

32.

Make a Joyful Noise

Focus: Laughter

For this adventure you'll need a tape recorder. Before you gather your family for prayer, tape each family member laughing for 10 to 15 seconds. This may test your joke-telling or tickling abilities! Leave a break of about five seconds between each person. Be sure to include yourself as well. Finish the tape with a segment that includes the entire family laughing together.

Gather family members together and have everyone sit around the tape recorder. Begin the time of prayer yourself by completing this prayer, "Lord, something you brought into my life that brings laughter and smiles is . . ." After you've completed this prayer, turn on the tape recorder and play the laughter of the first person you taped. When you come to the break, turn off the tape. Hearing the tape is sure to bring more laughter as family members recognize their own voices and guess as to who is laughing.

Then have another family member complete the same sentence prayer, thanking God for someone or something that has brought laughter and smiles to his or her life. After this person has prayed, play the voice of another family member laughing. Repeat this until each family member has prayed, and each voice has been heard laughing. When you've said "Amen," play the segment with the entire family laughing. Let your voices of merriment be a joyful sound to God!

Birds of Pray

Focus: We are important to God

For this adventure you'll need a bird feeder. If your family already owns one, fill it with birdseed. If not, consider purchasing a kit and assembling the feeder together as a family project. Or make one of the simple and easy-to-make feeders described below:

- Cut a hole in the side of an empty two-liter soft drink bottle to serve as a "door" for the birds. Fill the bottle up to this hole with bird seed. The bottle can be hung from the top with a string, or set on the ground in a patio or balcony area.

- Spread peanut butter into the crevices of a large pine cone. Roll the pine cone in bird seed until the peanut butter is covered. Hang this from a tree or awning.

Place your bird feeder in a location where you'll be able to see the birds without disturbing them. Then read this verse together: "Look at the birds of the air; they do not sow or reap or store away in barns, and yet your heavenly Father feeds them. Are you not much more valuable than they?" (Matthew 6:26).

Discuss the meaning of this verse together. Ask family members ways they know they're important to God (God sent Jesus, God forgives us, God provides for our needs, the Bible says so).

Then say, "Every time we see a bird at our feeder, let's stop to thank God that we're important to him."

Fill your bird feeder often, and as you enjoy the beauty of the creatures God has created, take time to thank God for creating and loving you!

Book of Answered Prayers

Focus: Recording prayers and praises

This adventure is a project for your family to work on over a long period of time. You'll need either a new notebook or a blank book, such as an unused journal.

Begin by asking family members to think of one or two prayers God has answered. This can be a recent answer to prayer, or one that happened years ago. Then have family members tell about these answers to prayer. After each person shares, write the details of the prayer and how it was answered in the book. Family members may want to write the information themselves, or one family member can be given the role of "scribe." Begin a new entry for each answered prayer.

When each person has made at least one entry into the book, begin interviewing other people about their answers to prayer:

- As guests join your family for a meal, ask them to share a time they remember God answering their prayers and record them in your family's book.

- Ask leaders from your church (such as pastors, Sunday school teachers, or volunteer staff members) to share answered prayers to be entered into your book.

- Talk with extended family members (grandparents, aunts and uncles, cousins, step-brothers or sisters, and so on) and include their answered prayers in the book.

• Ask any other friends or acquaintances you like!

As time goes by, your entries will begin to fill page after page with answers to prayer. Your own family members may want to continue adding their own answers to prayer as well. Occasionally read through some of the entries together as a reminder of how God has worked in the lives of many people over the course of many, many years!

"An answered prayer is a secondary miracle. The first miracle is prayer itself."

—Anonymous (overheard conversation)

35

Lucky Number Seven

Focus: Enemies

When you've gathered to pray together, read the following verse: "Then Peter came to Jesus and asked, 'Lord, how many times shall I forgive my brother when he sins against me? Up to seven times?' Jesus answered, 'I tell you, not seven times, but seventy-seven times'"(Matthew 18:21-22).

Explain that some translations of the Bible say seventy times seven instead of seventy-seven times. Either way, this is a lot of times! Discuss what this verse means. Have you ever forgiven one person that many times? Has someone had to forgive you that many times? Then read this verse aloud:

"But I tell you: Love your enemies and pray for those who persecute you" (Matthew 5:44).

Talk about how Jesus not only wants us to forgive people who make our lives difficult, but also how he wants us to love them and pray for them! Have each family member tell about one person that makes life difficult. This could be a bully at school, a "friend" who gossips behind your back, a boss or co-worker that makes work unpleasant, a neighbor who plays music too loud, or a teacher who seems to take pleasure in ridiculing you. Then ask family members how they feel about following God's instructions and praying for these "enemies."

Suggest that your family use the number seven (from seventy times seven or seventy-seven) as a reminder to pray for these people who make life harder. On every day of the month that has a seven in it (seventh, seventeenth, and twenty-seventh), join together in prayer for your enemies. Also take time during these prayer gatherings to share any ways you're finding these prayers answered. How is God changing this person, your attitude toward this person, you, or the situation? How is God helping you to love your enemies?

As time (and days with sevens in them) goes by, you may find yourself and other family members taking some of these "enemies" off of that list and adding them to your list of friends!

36

Heavenly Hallelujahs

Focus: "The Hallelujah Chorus"

For this adventure you'll need a recording of "The Hallelujah Chorus" from Handel's *Messiah*. If you don't own a copy of this, try your local library. It is often available on cassette or CD. If you decide to purchase a copy of the recording, we recommend *Handel's Young Messiah*, which is distributed by Word, Inc., and uses contemporary Christian artists.

Gather your family together and read the following information aloud:

In 1741, a man named Charles Jennens compiled different verses from the Bible that told the story of Jesus. He gave this collection to George F. Handel, a composer. Handel took only 24 days to write the music that accompanied these words. This was called *Messiah*. When Handel had written the part that is called "The Hallelujah Chorus," his servant found him with tears in his eyes. Handel had found such beauty in the words and music that he told his servant, "I think I did see all Heaven before me, and the great God himself!"

When *Messiah* was performed a few years later, the king of England attended a performance. He was so moved by "The Hallelujah Chorus" that he stood up and remained standing for the entire song. It was the custom that everyone stand when the king stands, so the entire audience stood for the chorus. This tradition has continued, and now it is customary to stand whenever you hear "The Hallelujah Chorus."

Have a family member read Revelation 11:15 and 19:6-7. Explain that the words of these verses are used in "The Hallelujah Chorus." Then discuss these questions with your family:

• What do these verses make you think about heaven?

• What do you think it will be like when we're all in heaven and singing praises to God?

Listen together to "The Hallelujah Chorus." Play it as loudly as you can! (You may stand if you like!) When the music is over, ask:

• How do you think these voices singing praise are like the voices of people in heaven singing to God?

• How does this music make you feel?

• How do you think God feels when he hears us singing praises to him like this?

Play the music again, and this time encourage family members to sing along as loudly as they like, praising God like the angels!

37

Little Reminders

Focus: Reminders to pray for each other

When your family comes together to pray, talk about how hard it can be to remember to pray for each other during the day. Then explain that you've found a fun way of reminding family members to pray for each other. Each day for the next week, you'll all be doing or wearing something in common. Whenever you notice these things, it will be a reminder to you to pray for other family members. Here are the reminders for the next week:

Day One:

Have each family member put an adhesive bandage on his or her knee (whether it's needed or not!). Each time you notice the bandage it will remind you to pray.

Day Two:

Draw a smiley face on the back of each person's hand as a reminder to pray.

Day Three:

Have family members lace their shoes backwards, so that the bow will be near the toes instead of near the ankles. (Those who wear Velcro hook-and-loop tape on their shoes can cross the straps into an X instead of pulling them straight across.) Each time a person looks at their feet they'll remember to pray!

Day Four:

Be sure each person has a small pebble to put into his or her pocket today. Feeling the pebble each time you reach into your pocket will bring family members to mind. Pray for them!

Day Five:

Ask everyone to wear the same color today (everyone wear green or everyone wear blue, for example). When the color catches your eye, remember to pray for your family.

Day Six:

Pin a safety pin to the sleeve of each family member as today's prayer reminder.

Day Seven:

Give each person a "friendship bracelet" to wear for the day. (Or tie a narrow ribbon or length of yarn around each wrist instead.) Each time you notice the bracelet, pray for your family members.

At the end of the week, ask family members how well the little reminders to pray worked. See if you can think of seven more little reminders to use another week!

A prayer of **Mother Teresa** of Calcutta....

"Dearest Lord, may I see you today and every day in the person of your sick, and whilst nursing them, minister unto you."

SOURCE: *Eerdman's Book of Famous Prayers*, compiled by Veronica Zundel, pg. 99, published by William B. Eerdman's Publishing Company.

Sin Slam Dunk

Focus: Forgiveness from each other and God

Provide blank paper and pens for your family. Have each person take a sheet of paper and write one or more things they've done that they'd like to ask forgiveness for. Younger family members can draw a picture or have another family member help them with the writing. Allow time for family members to write as many things as they want.

If you like, give family members the option of sharing the things they've written. If the need for forgiveness involves another family member, now is a good time to ask! For example, if Sarah had colored on the wall in Andrew's room, now is the time for her to say she's sorry and ask Andrew to forgive her. Or if Mom had yelled at Tenisha, she could take this opportunity to ask forgiveness. However, if family members aren't comfortable sharing, don't force them.

Now place a wastebasket in the center of the room. Stand together around the basket and have each person crumple his or her paper into a ball. Then pray together, asking God for forgiveness for the wrong things you've done. Encourage any family members who want to pray.

Then take turns "slam-dunking" your paper balls into the trash. When all the paper has made its way into the basket, join hands and thank God for "slam-dunking" the penalty of sin and for providing forgiveness.

Musical Prayers

Focus: Praying for each other

This adventure is similar to the game musical chairs, but every-one wins!

You'll need five pieces of paper in these colors: red, orange, blue, green, and brown. (If you don't have one or more of these colors, substitute another color and adjust the later directions as necessary.) The papers should be at least the size of a playing card, but they can be bigger if you like. If you have more than five members in your family, use two sheets papers of each color. You will also need a radio, tape recorder, or CD player.

Place the pieces of paper in a large circle on the floor. You may want to tape them to the floor to be sure they stay where they are put! Have each family member (including you) stand on a piece of paper. Then start the music.

While the music is playing have family members walk around the circle from paper to paper. When you stop the music, have each person stop on the paper closest to him or her. Then take turns praying as follows:

- If you are standing on red paper, pray for the adults in your family. This can include grandparents, aunts, uncles, and so on, as well as moms and dads.

- If you are standing on orange paper, pray for the person on your left.

- If you are standing on blue paper, pray for each child in your family. If you want, include cousins or family members not living with you (such as step-siblings or older children).

- If you're standing on green paper, pray for the person on your right.

- If you're standing on brown paper, pray for yourself!

After each person has prayed according to these guidelines, start the music again and start moving! When you stop the music, family members will be on different colors and can pray again according to their new color. Repeat the music and praying sequence as many times as you and your family want.

40.

Prayer for Heroes

Focus: People we admire

Before you come together for prayer, ask each family member to choose one person whom they admire or consider a hero. This could be a sports figure, singer, actor, politician, composer, scientist, teacher, and so on. If possible, have family members find an item that represents this person, such as their picture, a CD, or a copy of their latest book.

When you've gathered together, take turns telling about the person you admire. Share why this person is important to you and what you like about him or her.

After everyone has shared, take time to pray for each hero. If you know the person is a Christian, pray that he or she will grow stronger in faith and will continue to follow God. If they're not Christians, pray that they'll learn of God's love and accept his forgiveness. Pray for their families, careers, and the impact they have on those around them. Ask God to help these people use their position of popularity with the public for God's glory.

When you've prayed, take time to write to each person for whom you have prayed. In a brief note, express your admiration, and let this person know you're praying for him or her. If you'd like to hear back from this person, include your name and address (a self-addressed, stamped envelope is always helpful too).

If you don't know the address to send your letters to, check the library for these or similar books:

- *The Address Book: How to Reach Anyone Who is Anyone,* by Michael Levine, published by Perigree Books.

- *Star Guide,* published by Axiom Information Resources

If these sources don't list the person you're praying for, try sending your correspondence in care of a larger organization with which this person is affiliated. This may be the recording label for a musician (the address is often on the cassette or CD case), the team of a sports figure, the publisher of an author, and so on. Even if you can't locate an address, keep praying for this person. God knows where they are!

A prayer of **Teresa of Avila** . . . .

"From silly devotions and from sour-faced saints, good Lord deliver us."

SOURCE: *Berdman's Book of Famous Prayers*, compiled by Veronica Zundel, pg. 51, published by William B. Berdman's Publishing Company.

41.

Gone with the Wind

Focus: *Saying you're sorry*

For this adventure you'll need a handful of balloons. You may use helium balloons if you like, but ones that you inflate yourself will work just as well.

Give each family member a balloon and a pen (permanent markers work best). Ask each person to think of something they've done wrong that they'd like God to forget about. Tell them to write one or two words on the balloon to represent what they've done. For example, if Emma is sorry she called Jared a mean name, she might write "mean name" on her balloon. If Kadeem is sorry he took Dad's car without asking, he could write "took car." Have older family members help those who cannot write yet.

When everyone is ready, have different family members volunteer to read the following verses aloud:

- "As far as the east is from the west, so far has he removed our transgressions from us" (Psalm 103:12).

- "If we confess our sins, he is faithful and just and will forgive us our sins and purify us from all unrighteousness" (1 John 1:9).

Be sure all family members know the meanings of words such as transgressions, confess, just, purify, and unrighteousness. Discuss together what these verses mean.

Then begin a time of prayer, asking God for forgiveness according to what is written on your balloon. After you've prayed, pop your balloon with a thumbtack or pin to represent the forgiveness of your sin. Then pass the pin to another family member and allow him or her to pray then pop his or her

80

balloon. Continue until all balloons have been popped. Ask family members how popping your balloon is like sins being gone. How is it different?

Close by thanking God for being true to his word and forgiving our sins.

Luke 18:10-14 records this parable Jesus told about prayer. . .

"Two men went up to the temple to pray, one a Pharisee and the other a tax collector. The Pharisee stood up and prayed about himself: 'God, I thank you that I am not like other men—robbers, evildoers, adulterers—or even like this tax collector. I fast twice a week and give a tenth of all I get.'

"But the tax collector stood at a distance. He would not even look up to heaven, but beat his breast and said, 'God, have mercy on me, a sinner.'

"I tell you that this man, rather than the other, went home justified before God. For everyone who exalts himself will be humbled, and he who humbles himself will be exalted."

42

Stations of Prayer

Focus: Different kinds of prayer

Before your family gathers for a time of prayer, determine four separate areas of your home that can be used for prayer. This could be the four corners of a room, or four separate rooms. These will be four prayer "stations." At each station, place a piece of paper with one of the following words written on it:

- Praise
- Thanks
- Request
- Confession

When your family comes together to pray, explain that you'll be taking time individually to pray at the different prayer stations in your home. Show family members where these are and tell what to do at each station, following this guide:

- At the Praise station, tell God why you think he's wonderful! Say a prayer or sing a song of praise.

- At the Thanks station, thank God for what he's done.

- At the Request station, tell God your needs and the needs of others.

- At the Confession station, tell God you're sorry for things you've done wrong and ask him to forgive you.

Have each family member go to a different station. (If your family has more than four members, two people can be at the same station, but ask them to pray individually.) Explain that everyone will stay at that station and pray as directed there for two to three minutes. (You can make this time shorter if you have younger children, or longer if you have older children.)

Begin your time of prayer. After two minutes (or whatever amount of time you have decided upon) has passed, have everyone change to a new station. Again, pray at the stations for the allotted time, then repeat the process until each person has had a chance to pray at each station.

Note: If one or more of your children are under age four, this adventure can be done with the entire family together at each station, or an adult can visit each station with the child to guide him or her in prayer.

"Lord, teach us to pray. Some of us are not skilled in the art of prayer. As we draw near to Thee in thought, our spirits long for Thy Spirit, and reach out for Thee, longing to feel Thee near."

—**Peter Marshall**, former chaplain of the United States Senate

SOURCE: *The Prayers of Peter Marshall*, edited by Catherine Marshall, pg. 15, published in 1989 by the McGraw-Hill Book Company.

43.

Finger Prayer

Focus: A child's prayer

Small children will enjoy this finger play that guides them through a time of prayer. Use it with your whole family, letting the younger children lead!

• My thumb is smallest it's plain to see. It's a reminder to pray for me!

• My pointing finger shows me where to go. I'll pray for those who guide me as I grow.

• My middle finger stands so tall, I'll thank God because he watches over all.

• Finger number four is weaker than the rest. Please God, care for those who need your rest.

• My very last finger is tiny like a child. I'll pray for other kids across the whole world wide.

As your family recites each line together and refers to the indicated finger, stop for a moment to pray as directed by the rhyme.

44.

Outside-In Prayer

Focus: Family

Join together in the largest room of your house or apartment. Have family members stand against the walls, as far from each other as possible. Explain that after each thing that you pray about, everyone should take a large step toward the center of the room. Use these ideas for things to pray about:

- Praise God for creating families.

- Ask God to forgive family members when they don't treat each other well.

- Ask God to help family members show kindness to each other.

- Thank God for sending Jesus to help us all know how to treat each other.

- Ask God to help family members be examples of Jesus' love to each other every day.

As soon as everyone in your family has stepped to the middle of the room, join together in a family group hug and close your time by thanking God for each person that makes up your special family.

45

Instrument of Prayer

Focus: Peace

Read the following prayer attributed to St. Francis of Assisi aloud to your family:

Lord, make me an instrument of your peace.
Where there is hatred, let me sow love,
Where there is injury, pardon,
Where there is doubt, faith,
Where there is despair, hope,
Where there is darkness, light,
Where there is sadness, joy.

O Divine Master, grant that I may not so much seek
to be consoled as to console,
not so much to be understood as to understand,
not so much to be loved, as to love;
for it is in giving that we receive,
it is in pardoning that we are pardoned,
it is in dying, that we awake to eternal life.

After reading the prayer, discuss what it means to different family members. Then ask:

• The person praying this prayer asks God to make him or her an instrument of God's peace. What kind of "instrument" do you think the writer meant?

• How can you be an instrument of peace?

Have each person think of a tool or instrument that could be used to show peace, or that might represent peace. For example, a hammer could be an instrument of peace if it represents building up others. A wind chime could represent sounds of harmony. A rope might bind people together in unity. Let each person think of one item that represents the instrument of peace he or she would like to be. If possible, have family members actually go and get the item they are thinking of. Then let each person explain how their instrument represents peace.

Take turns praying. Ask each person to pray that God would make them an instrument like the one they have chosen. For example, "Lord, help me to be like these ear plugs. They make things quiet, and I want to be quiet when I think about you." When everyone has prayed, again read the prayer of St. Francis aloud as your closing prayer and request.

"And knowledge about prayer to a loving God can ward off frenzied efforts to 'muster up faith' in hopes of impressing God—prayer does not work that way, as the Bible shows. God is already full of loving concern; we do not need to impress him with spiritual calisthenics."

—Philip Yancey

SOURCE: *The Inspirational Study Bible*, edited by Max Lucado, pg. 581, published in 1995 by Word Bibles.

46

Far from Home

Focus: Remembering others in prayer

Use this prayer adventure when a family member will be away from home for several days. It could be used when a parent is away on a business trip, when a child spends a week at camp, during those first nervous days of school, or any other time when family members will be separated for a length of time.

Bring your family together and remind everyone of the upcoming separation. Then read the following passages together:

- I thank God, whom I serve, as my forefathers did, with a clear conscience, as night and day I constantly remember you in my prayers (2 Timothy 1:3).

- I always thank my God as I remember you in my prayers, because I hear about your faith in the Lord Jesus and your love for all the saints (Philemon 1:4-5).

- I have not stopped giving thanks for you, remembering you in my prayers (Ephesians 1:16).

Then ask your family these questions:

- Why do you think it's important to pray for each other when we're apart?

- How do you feel when you know someone far away is praying for you?

- As our family experiences time apart from each other, what are things we should remember to pray about?

(For example, safety during travel, freedom from fear while at camp, or whatever the needs are in your specific situation.)

Together determine one or more specific times during the day for everyone to remember to pray. Choose a time when family members can be reminded to pray by an alarm or bell of some kind. For example, your family might choose to pray at 10:15 A.M. One child will be reminded to pray because a school bell rings at this time. Mom can set the alarm on her computer at work, Dad has an alarm on his digital watch, and another child will be reminded by the chiming of the clock at home. Use any alarms or time signals you can think of. Set needed alarms now so everyone will be reminded. Then have everyone commit to pray for the needs you've discussed when the bells start ringing the next day.

If your time of separation is only one day, you may want to be reminded to pray several times through the day. If the time apart will be lengthy, have only one or two prayer reminders each day.

When the family is reunited, talk about how everyone felt knowing that others were praying at the same time during the day. How did you see your specific prayers answered?

"Pray for me, and I'll pray for you."

—Michael W. Smith

SOURCE: Song—"Pray for Me," by Michael W. Smith and Wayne Kirkpatrick, published in *The Group Songbook*, song #89.

Prayer Adventures for Special Occasions

47

Birthday Candle Prayers

Focus: Birthdays

Start this new tradition on the next birthday of a family member.

When you're ready to sing "Happy Birthday" and have the birthday boy or girl (or mom, dad, grandparent, or whomever!) blow out the candles, stop for a moment and ask each person to think silently of something they're thankful for about the person celebrating today. Then, as you light each candle, have people take turns praying out loud a short, one-sentence prayer of thanks about the birthday person.

For example, if Dillon is turning eight, family members might say,

- "God, thanks that Dillon has lots of energy."

- "Thank you for Dillon's happy smile."

- "Lord, I'm glad for Dillon's helpful attitude."

- "I'm thankful that Dillon gives great hugs."

- "Thanks for sending Dillon to our family!"

When eight prayers (one for each candle) have been offered, go ahead and sing "Happy Birthday" and have the child blow out the candles.

This tradition can be carried on for every family member, no matter how old or young. However, once you get into the teen years and above, you may find it safer to pray before lighting the candles—unless you are fast pray-ers or have tall candles!

Option: This prayer adventure may also be used to celebrate Baptism anniversaries. Light a baptismal candle to remember and rejoice at new birth.

48.

Letters to God

Focus: Advent or New Year's

The beginning of a new year is a good time to evaluate where you've been and what your goals for the coming year are. This adventure could be used at any time, but we suggest using it to kick off a new calendar year. It could also be used at the beginning of Advent, the start of a new church year.

As you come together to pray, explain that we can communicate to God by writing our thoughts to him. Give each person paper and pen and say, "Let's begin the new year by writing letters of prayer to God!"

Ask family members to write areas where they need help from God, things they'd like to thank God for, and so on. Children who cannot write may draw a picture expressing their thoughts to God, or have an older family member help them.

When each person has completed his or her letter, give everyone the opportunity to read the letters aloud in prayer. If family members are uncomfortable with this, have everyone read their letters silently in quiet prayer.

Then have each person seal his or her letter in an envelope, writing names and the dates on the outside. Gather the envelopes and place them in a file, drawer, or other place for safekeeping. Make a notation on your calendar, one year from today's date, to get the letters out and give them to each family member. (If you're a bit forgetful, you might want to also note where you've stored the letters!)

When the year has passed, gather family members together again and distribute each letter of prayer to its owner. Let family members open the letters and read their prayers from a year ago. Then take time to share how prayers have been answered, how situations have changed, and how God is still working in the areas mentioned in each letter. Take time to thank God for what he's done in each life, and pray for continued support with ongoing concerns. You might even want to write new letters to God to save for another year!

"I said to the man who stood at the gate of the Year,
'Give me a light that I may tread safely into the unknown.'
And he replied, 'Go out into the darkness and put your hand into the hand of God. That shall be to you better than light and safer than a known way.'"

SOURCE: *Against the Night*, by Charles Colson, pg. 181, published in 1989 by Servant Publications.

49

Out of the Darkness

Focus: Good Friday or Easter

Have your family squeeze together into the smallest and darkest space your home has to offer. If you can fit, a closet is the best. Or if you family is larger, a dark bathroom will work.

When you're all together, tell about Jesus' death on the cross and how he was buried in a dark tomb. (If you need a refresher on the details of this story, read the account given in Mark 15:21-47 before gathering your family.) Explain that just

as the tomb was without light, our hearts are without light when Jesus isn't there. Ask family members to think of things that make our hearts dark and without light. Then pray together that God would remove these things from your lives.

Then remind your family that Jesus arose from the dead! (Find the details in Mark 16.) Let the youngest family member open the door and release you all from the dark. After you've untangled yourselves from the cramped darkness, tell about how Jesus rose from the dead and brought light into our lives. Then spend a few minutes thanking God for sending Jesus, for bringing him back to life, and for giving us life because of his love!

Matthew 26:36-41 records this story of prayer . . .

"Then Jesus went with his disciples to a place called Gethsemane, and he said to them, 'Sit here while I go over there and pray.' He took Peter and the two sons of Zebedee along with him, and he began to be sorrowful and troubled. Then he said to them, 'My soul is overwhelmed with sorrow to the point of death. Stay here and keep watch with me.'

"Going a little further, he fell with his face to the ground and prayed, 'My Father, if it is possible, may this cup be taken from me. Yet not as I will, but as you will.'

"Then he returned to his disciples and found them sleeping. 'Could you men not keep watch with me for one hour?' he asked Peter. 'Watch and pray so that you will not fall into temptation. The spirit is willing, but the body is weak.'"

50.

Star-Spangled Prayer

Focus: Independence Day

This adventure can be used any time of year, but we think it goes well with July 4 (Independence Day). You'll need a United States flag for this adventure. (If you can't find the real thing, a picture of a flag will work, too.)

As your family comes together for prayer, ask if anyone knows the meaning of the stars and stripes on the flag. If not, explain that each star represents one of the 50 states in the Union and that each of the stripes represents one of the original thirteen colonies. The colors of the flag also have meaning. Red symbolizes courage, white is for purity, and blue represents justice.

As you examine and discuss the flag, explain to your family that you'd like to use the flag and its symbolism as a guide to prayer. Join together in talking and praying as follows:

- For every star on the flag, think of something your family is thankful for. As you think of each reason to give thanks, have different family members offer a one-sentence prayer of thanksgiving. For example, "Thank you that we are free to worship you in our country," or "Thanks, God, for giving us food each day," and so on. Continue until you've thanked God 50 times. (You may want to use this part of the adventure over the course of several days or a week.)

- As the blue field behind the stars represents justice, pray for people who are oppressed and in need of justice. This could be people in the United States who don't receive justice such as hungry children or people who are treated unfairly. You may want to include people in other countries who don't enjoy the freedoms we do in America. You could also pray that we would continue to be allowed to exercise these freedoms.

- For each of the six white stripes on the flag, ask God to bring purity to a different area of your lives. This might include purity of speech toward each other, purity in actions to each other, and so on.

- Pray for courage as guided by the seven red stripes of the flag. A family member may need courage to stand up for his or her beliefs at school or work, or you may all need courage to share about God's love to an unfriendly neighbor.

Close your time together by praying for America, asking God to bring guidance and show his love to all who live under this flag.

Variation: If you live in a country other than the United States, use your flag and a national holiday to create a prayer adventure similar to this one. Research the symbols and colors used in your national flag and together determine ways to use these as a guide for prayer. Consider the specific needs of your country as well as reasons you are thankful for your country.

51.

Travel Time with God

Focus: Summer Vacation

Use this adventure the next time your family is on a road trip or a driving vacation.

• Every time you see cattle, thank God for a different person in the car, and tell one reason you're glad this person is along on the journey.

• When you see a sign for a rest stop, sing a hymn or chorus of a praise song. (In some cases, "The Hallelujah Chorus" may be appropriate!)

• Each time you pass a mile-marker ending in 00 (such as 100, 200, and so on), pray for the driver of your car. Ask God to keep this person alert and to give guidance as he or she drives the car.

• Be on the lookout for one fast-food restaurant chain. When that restaurant is seen, thank God for the friends or family you'll be seeing on this trip.

You can add to these suggestions to fit the needs and interests of your family. For example, every time you see a license plate from a certain state, pray for a specific request. Or each time you see a sign with a particular color on it, thank God for a specific person or belonging. Use this prayer adventure as often as you like during your trip, letting family members change the items to look for and the prayers to go with them.

52

Christmas Card Prayer

Focus: Remembering friends after Christmas

This Christmas, when you're taking down the decorations, set aside all the cards and newsletters your family received. Place these in a basket, napkin-holder, or even a bright box. Set the container on or near your dining room table.

Each evening during dinner, take the top card from the stack and tell your family who sent the card. As a family, talk about the person or family who sent the card and let family members share current information about what is happening with this individual or family.

For example, you might know now that the person no longer is looking for a job as had been indicated in a newsletter. Or a child might know that the friend who gave her this card is sick this week. You could also take time to let family members tell of special memories they have of this person or family.

When you're ready, pray for the individual or family who sent the card or newsletter. Mention specific praises or needs depending or your knowledge of what they are. Then return the card to the bottom of the stack.

In your own Christmas cards and letters, let people know your family will be remembering and praying for others during the next year. It might just increase the number of cards you receive!

"Humor is a prelude to faith, and laughter is the beginning of prayer."

—Reinhold Neibuhr

SOURCE: *Making Merry*, by Kathy Bubel, published in 1995 by Release Ink, pg. 13.

Index of Scripture References

Old Testament

reference	page	reference	page
Joshua 24:15b	44	Psalm 66:1-4	54
1 Samuel 2:2	27	Psalm 86:11	28
2 Samuel 7:22	27	Psalm 103:12	80
Psalm 5:1-2	39	Psalm 122	19
Psalm 9:1-2	26	Psalm 139:1-4, 7-12	53
Psalm 25:1-5	26	Psalm 145:1-2	28
Psalm 42:1-2a	27	Amos 5:24	27
Psalm 51:10,12	28	Habakkuk 3:2	27
Psalm 61:1-3	28		

New Testament

reference	page	reference	page
Matthew 5:43-48	19	Luke 18:10-14	81
Matthew 5:44	68	Romans 1:20	30
Matthew 6:5-8	20	Ephesians 1:16	88
Matthew 6:9b-13	26	Ephesians 3:14-17a	27
Matthew 6:26	65	Ephesians 3:17b-19	27
Matthew 9:35-38	20	2 Thessalonians 3:1-2	20
Matthew 18:21-22	68	2 Timothy 1:3	88
Matthew 26:36-41	97	Philemon 1:4-5	88
Mark 13:32-37	19	Hebrews 13:18	20
Mark 15:2-47	96	James 5:13-16	14
Mark 16	97	James 5:16b-18	37
Luke 6:27-36	19	1 John 1:9	80
Luke 11:1-4	58	Revelation 11:15	71
Luke 18:1-8	20	Revelation 19:6-7	71